Tender Skin &
Heavy Limbs

Tender Skin & Heavy Limbs

Misti Rae

 iUniverse®

TENDER SKIN & HEAVY LIMBS

iUniverse books may be ordered through booksellers or by contacting:

iUniverse
1663 Liberty Drive
Bloomington, IN 47403
www.iuniverse.com
844-349-9409

ISBN: 978-1-6632-3538-1 (sc)
ISBN: 978-1-6632-3539-8 (e)

Library of Congress Control Number: 2021924927

Print information available on the last page.

iUniverse rev. date: 01/26/2022

To my love

Thank you for inspiring me to share my past and my writing

I hope to write something beautiful about you someday

I find it hard to breathe

sometimes

like I lost the ability to collapse my lungs

or expand my lungs

and I write poems about it

sometimes

and then I speak every word as if I'm out of breath when really

I just refuse to breathe

sometimes

and I know it's weird not wanting oxygen

but waiting to gasp until I can't take it anymore

is erotic

sometimes

trust me

when I tell you there is more power in my breath than the words I say

sometimes

I have so much sadness I've turned some

into rage

Threading tragedy into beautifully arranged stories

I want to be uncomfortable

I want to be startling

I want to be shocking

If you read what I write and feel your heart is being ripped out

And shoved back in

Then I've done all that I have planned to do

I want to write lines of gold filigree
Poems that wrap around you tightly
Every word a gentle caress to your soul

I want to bleed your heart
In the most tasteful way possible
Every pause a new tear in an artery

I want to fight and attack the universe
The vast lightyears of space or just the fabric we live in
Everything I've written down as a challenge to my existence

I want to want things
Even things that don' t matter or make sense
I'll learn to want
And crave
And desire

But I was born to hunger
The code that writes beauty
Oh, my sweet poetry

I'm writing in pencil
so my mistakes feel like ink so permanent
on my skin
Ink so permanent I can't cross out, erase, or delete it

I'm writing in pencil
so my words don't bleed the page I write on
Bleed the page like drops of water
seeping into the fabric of your clothes

I'm trying to write in pencil
Yet the words that come to mind have
little meaning to them

Maybe it's time I wrote in pen

Every time the pen hits the paper tonight I blank
I'm stuck trying to write words when,
Usually all I write is feelings that turn into words
Every time the pen hits the paper tonight
I want to drag the pen so deep it rips the paper
I want to do it over and over
Until the paper is left in shreds
I don't want to write
I don't want to feel
Every time the pen hits

When deeper peace settles into my skin
I hope it is when I've caught life some meaning

When joyous delirium seeps into my skin
I hope it eases away the sadness in my struggling

When I'm all but empty
I hope my story is filled to the very last page

I used to have moments when I noticed
The sky is really beautiful and,
although I know that I am often sad,
I might fall in love with the world
And adore all the oxygen inside my lungs
And not feel scared anymore

Those moments have become few and fleeting
I'm always sad
And the oxygen in my lungs is stuck
Because of the panic inside my brain
And right now
Even though I know the sky is really beautiful
I am afraid

I have somewhat of a love affair with the sky
And I'm not gonna lie
We have a lot in common, she and I
A sad soul and cerulean eyes
We've seen many days & many nights
Always there yet very far
Something to stare at
Something to forget
Full of light even when dark
No, it's not a lie
Don't we have a lot in common
Me and the sky

I have no money

I have a terrible job

Almost everything makes me sad nowadays

Even when I'm happy I'm not sure if I'm really feeling it

For human beings so smart I really think we still don't understand life

I don't mean to say money is everything

And I don't mean to say work is everything

But most of all I don't think happiness is everything

I used to think it was but now I think

Everything is everything

I lost weight again
Lost it to the sadness
Call it sickness if you want
I'm thin, weak, meaningless
Inside and out
I seep through the cracks in the world
And I know I'll find my weight in this world again
But for now I'm going to stay here
Losing weight
And seeping through
The cracks

I try to cut a path to where I want to be in this life
Yet I always seem to cut myself
A shock to my system this unexpected outcome

This wasn't the journey I was hoping for
I just hope I still reach my goal

Maybe instead of trying to cut my way
I should make my way with something less damaging

I'll make a path on the pages of words
This will be a stunning odyssey

Any cuts will be battle scars
My new path will be the bandages
And the healing ointment the words

I keep repeating myself
Like the devil whispering in your ear
But I'm not whispering
I'm yelling at you
Like an angel refusing to give up hope
Waiting for you to say the right thing
Or the hallelujah
But you are human
And I am not holy
Selfish mixed with selfless
Giving mixed with greed
Hopeless mixed with hopeful
I am just as human as you
So I keep repeating myself
Wishing and waiting
For you to understand

It's weird how I have all these ideas about you wrapped up in my head
I know you like to laugh & joke
And I know you love ice cream even when I don't
I know you like to be outside
And you don't mind getting dirt under your nails
I know every day you will try to keep me on my toes
I know you will look at me not just for
My lips
My legs
My hair
Or my skin
You will look at me as if you see everything that I am
It's weird but years from now I will tell you about all these ideas
I had
Of you
Just wrapped up
In my head

I can't remember the last time
I lit a fire and watched as the smoke & embers ascended
into the night sky

But in this moment
As you walk away from me
And all the warmth leaves with you
I'm reminded of smoke & embers

These phantoms are trying to kill me
I don't know how they keep finding me
I don't know how to make them leave
A constant battle of trying to get free
A constant reminder they still won't leave me be
Haunting me to the brink of death
Making me hate my immortality
Because even though I seem awake
I am already dead
And these phantoms are made up in my head
I'm getting destroyed here
So let me tell you my dear
I don't know a lot of things
But I can say
These phantoms are trying to kill me

I can't explain why or how I came to care
at all
But I do care
I can't tell you why or how I still do after all
I went through
But I still do
I can't figure out why or how I'm losing sleep even when I'm not
thinking about you
But I'm losing it
I can't say why or how I feel like I can't walk away from you
But I can't
Why is it so hard for you to get over someone?
How is it I have the same problem?

I too,

enjoy abusive relationships

He calls me stupid and an idiot but,

He says 'good morning beautiful'

Every morning

He tells me all the reasons I'm not good enough

Like how I speak too much

Or sleep too much

Now I don't sleep at all but,

He holds me tight every night

He says I don't care about him or do enough for him

I should've stayed

Because next time I go

I might not come back to him but,

I too,

Enjoy abusive relationships

And no matter the pain

I cling to the love

For hope that I am enough

I smell beer on their breath
and they're slurring their words
they promised they would stop drinking
too much
And lately I've learned not to hope
too much
Why do I care
so much
about someone
so lost
so broken down
so gone

Nope, not gonna happen
This again
Telling me I can't do something
Or telling me I can't have something
I know *life isn't fair*
But I've asked and I've worked for it
And before you said you would say yes
If I did one thing for you
Now you say I must do more
I wish you would just say no
Keep me abused but at least then I won't be used
A liar, manipulator, reason for my pain
But I'm glad I learned early in life
I shouldn't have others tell me shit
Yes, I have to go for it myself

He touched me
And it was just a touch
One that wrote lines upon lines
Of poetry on every inch of my skin
And when he spoke
Just to speak
Black liquid oozed from his lips like oil making me sick
From all the lies
And the sin

He loved taking pictures of me
I loved it too
I used to feel beautiful and special
And unbreakable
Now even looking at myself in the mirror is impossible
He loved taking pictures of me
He said is favorite one was the one I'm half naked in
The one with black lace against pale skin
The one that I'm looking into his camera and biting my lip in
He loved taking pictures of me
But I hate that picture
The one I'm half naked in
I can still feel the stale cold air of the room on my skin
And when I look at that picture
I can see the pained look in my wide eyes

He's yelling at me again
He wants nothing more than to call me the problem and have me fixed
What problem am I? What is my problem?
He wants to beat me down again
He wants me to do what he wants
when he wants
how he wants
I will fight back
He is not the puppet master
I am not his puppet

He paints me with all the colors I despise

I am nothing but a thoughtless, caring person
Yet he paints me with red and I seem to be
a stupid selfish bitch
If I thought only of myself, I would be gone in a puff of smoke
Because I am nothing more than the people I care about
Yet he paints me with grey and I seem to
care about nothing
I seem to be
nothing
I am nothing but my own work of art
Yet he paints me with brown and as you look at his depiction of me
you miss the fact that you can no longer see
my true colors

He paints me with all the colors I despise

I'll regret it if I do this
And I'll regret it if I don't do that
It affects you
So you think it best to tell me what to do
But you affect me too

I want what is best for me, that no longer includes you

You'll regret putting constraints on me
You forgot I was a person
And put constraints on everything
No relationship can survive restricted access
I prioritize myself because,
It's clear you can't care about me
As much as
I care about
You

You can't spend your whole life
keeping all your deepest thoughts to yourself
   And you think
It's easier not to move
         not to breathe
         not to think
in front of everyone else
So many times before you've been
told by someone to stop
            to just thinking your thoughts
            to just stop feeling that way
          because it's not right
          because you're wrong
          because you shouldn't feel that way
And now you're told to ignore it all
      that they're wrong
      that they shouldn't have made you feel that way
      that you shouldn't have let them
But the thing is
Other people can tell you anything and it won't matter
Unless you choose to believe them

You and your inflated sense of self importance
You constantly gaslight me into thinking I'm never right and you're always right
You belittle my emotions making me think that I'm too sensitive
Am I wrong to feel how I feel?
Your denial of what happened makes me wonder if I am crazy
I'm angry and scared and never sure what to do
I've had to learn to accept my own feelings as my truth—
No matter who says they are wrong
My boundaries have evicted you from my life
But you are the narcissist that still lives in my head
Even after all this time it still feels invalidating but I am strong now—
And you are no longer allowed to be here

Maybe you see it as water to throw under the bridge, again
But that doesn't mean I don't get to see it as water still drowning me
A two-way street that has a one-way sign
You think that just because you say something we all have to believe it
Maybe my head is way up in the clouds
But that doesn't mean I don't know the color of grass is green

You say the grass can bend, but it is straight
And I say it is not straight, but grass can be bent
I'm not wrong
I'm not arguing
I'm not lying
I'm say the same thing differently

Maybe that makes you see me wrong
Because in your eyes I can't see "right"
I still don't understand how else to tell you it hurts

You are incapable of love
yelling back and forth
slamming doors
and silence
is all I have learned
the little spaces in time
where happiness lives
always becoming fewer and fewer
now I prefer to be alone so you can't hurt me
and then dress it up as love
You care about me
so you hit me
for speaking
slam me against the wall
for walking away
and call me useless
for not doing it your way
If this is really love
I don't want it
I am incapable of love
yelling back and forth
slamming doors
and silence
is all I have learned

Don't be quick to anger

How can you say that?

No, you chained me down and tore my wings from me

My skin

My bone

Exposed

Searing pain I do not have words to describe

Don't be quick to anger

No, you caged me forever by mutilating my being

Making me less than holy

Don't be quick to anger

How can you say that?

The ground will shake, and I will strike you down

You will be nothing

For I am not quick to anger

But my ire is strong enough to devour the heavens

And make your hell

I want to throw away all the things that cause me pain

Screaming and fighting to move them away

And make them leave

It's harder to do as you say

And just walk away

Because it clings to you

And you could be walking

For miles or days

Even years you might say

So I'll meet you at the end

And you'll hear my screams and my battles

I'll earn my victory

My peace

With sweat and more pain

It will feed my fire that will keep me warm

I choose fight and you choose flight

So I hope you aren't too cold

Standing in a field of daisies
wishing for lilacs instead
You've been there in a trance
for a couple of days
You never feel the warmth of the sun
when it raises in the sky
You don't hear anything around you
or feel the wind on your skin
All this nothing is starting to hurt
Soon you'll turn to stone in that field
of daisies

Unpack your tragedy

What skeletons are pretending to be ghosts?

I woke up one day—older and with more to drag around

Who the fuck decided these will be my skeletons?

The trauma was painful enough

Why does it feel like it won't go ever away?

In a daze and zoning out

What will help me cope with life?

I thought I was better than woke but I'm still lost

Who the fuck decided how to exist?

Not ready to unpack my tragedy

What lets me tell you to unpack yours?

I went to battle
Of a special kind
Every word I know
Sharpened into obsidian shards
I went to battle
My sword drawn
Armor shining in the setting sun
Tints of red in the sky adding to the lust for blood
I went to battle
And found
My words don't do the damage I was hoping for
I went to battle
And lost my mind
Every hurt I can't forgive myself for
Every time

The silence gets to me
with the hum of the air
and the absolute stillness o the air
but tonight the silence is loud
with voices in the next room

my eyes keep closing on their own
nothingness will reach me
before any noise

Watching as the bumble bee dizzily flies around her head
She hears it's constant buzzing and slips into her soft bed
She closes her eyes and sees images of dancing goldfish
The lilacs in the garden growing and expanding like bacteria in a petri dish
Standing in green grass fields bathed in setting golden light
Sitting in a small living room looking at everything in black and white
She's in a dark room where even the pitch-dark shadows smile at her
She's running frightened and trying to hide but she can still hear them whisper
Breathing hard and still running in the dark she is filled with dread
The pounding of her feet sounding louder and louder is now the throbbing of her head

When my blood runs cold
and the rivers run red
Will someone please tell me
if I truly am dead
Because not fully knowing
is causing confusion in my head
He forces his way in and closes the door
Now he's in my bed
I feel my blood run cold
But, honey, it's his blood making the river red
So tell me
Am I the one dead?

The moonlight doesn't ask
And the walls don't watch
The trees don't dance
And the wind doesn't speak
These things are no more real than the words floating from my mind
And onto this page
They don't happen anywhere but inside someone's mind

What is this blind leap of faith you are asking me to take?

I've jumped into the abyss for you one too many times

A cyclops of lies and a pit of untrustworthy vipers

What's telling you this time I'll land without a scratch to my soul?

I've felt a sting and I've heard the words too many times

A soul such as mine can only last a few washes in the river

What is it that proves to me trusting you is ok?

I cannot tell you—

So if you want me to jump

Maybe you could show me—

Somehow light up this dark abyss

Until I can see safety at the bottom

She sees through stained glass windows
Silvery sweet music fills her mind
Her smile starts to liquefy your heart
And her laugh has become your favorite sound
She only looks at you through rose colored glasses
You love everything about her
At least on the surface

His lips or his touch on my bare skin
Does not define me
The way he talks to me or makes love to me
Does not define him

Yes

His touch makes it hard to breathe
And his words make me smile
His worries make me worry
And his actions sometimes make me frown

I see him hold his breath around me
And I see how I create his smile
I see how I cause problems
And I see his actions how no one else can

Still, the way he loves me
And the way I love him
It's hard to want anyone else

So I've had a glimpse of who you could be
And you were beautiful
Your smooth radiating waves of kindness
And clear sensibilities
Bathing you in fireless phoenix lighting
So maybe this was the purest notion of you

So I've had a glimpse of who you could be
And you aren't that perfect
You're not always kind
And sometimes it is hard to be sensible
Your soul was dipped in imperfection
So maybe this is the exact notion of you that is true and meant to be

She was damned to live
as her head slammed down on the floor
she tried to get up, to get away
but he brought his hand down across
her cheek

She was damned
feeling helpless and weak
as he slammed her head down on the floor
her head was pounding, vision blurring
she was trying to keep it from fading to black
but he brought his hand down

She was crying and begging for it to stop
as he held her neck in a tight vice grip
leaving marks on her tender skin
she cried and said stop, cried and said sorry
but he called her a useless bitch and a whore
then told her to shut up and stop crying

She was crying hurting and feeling terrified
as he held her in a tight vice grip
leaving marks
her eyes squeezed shut, holding her tears

She was crying
but she tried to stop and be quiet
trying to listen to him, to not make it last longer
Then he shouted whore and useless bitch

She was motionless on the floor
as her tears dried and the pain continued throbbing through her body
she was trying not to think, trying to feel numb
but she couldn't help thinking of everything he said
every hit

She was motionless, where he left her
the heaviness of her limbs weighing her down
she was trying to forget
watching the dust settle on the carpet
but she couldn't
she would never forget